In Rositta Joseph's hands, poetry engages deftly with the world's despair and angst, conjuring a balm that is as precious as it is potent, and as capable of compounding insight as it is of begetting light. Sweeping across sentiments and visions that range from the personal to the social and from the mundane to the mythic, these poems assert their worth by a steady command over language, an honest plumbing of emotions, a clear vision of life's complexities, and a bold foray into the intricacies of philosophical negotiation. Should the world, again, betray, will there be revenge? For Rositta, these poems are both retribution and resurrection--an awakening in poetry that we are thrilled to witness.

*Dr. Basudhara Roy*

Rositta Joseph Valiyamattam's collection of sixty-three poems blows like a fresh morning breeze over a landscape littered with pretentious approximations of poetry – the curse of modernism and postmodernism. The greats of modernist and postmodernist poetry indeed did a great disservice – they spawned poet pretenders who believe that fragments make poems. These poems proliferate on the printed page and the internet – mere words, without feelings. That's where Rositta's poems mark a departure. Her lines are expressions of deeply felt emotions, and they tug at the heartstrings of the reader. The contemporary merge seamlessly into the eternal and the mythical into the topical. This slim volume is definitely one for keeps!

*Dr. Sangeetha Puthiyedath*

# A Poet's Promise

Rositta Joseph

BLACK EAGLE BOOKS
Dublin, USA | Bhubaneswar, India

Black Eagle Books
USA address:
7464 Wisdom Lane
Dublin, OH 43016

India address:
E/312, Trident Galaxy, Kalinga Nagar,
Bhubaneswar-751003, Odisha, India

E-mail: info@blackeaglebooks.org
Website: www.blackeaglebooks.org

First International Edition Published by
Black Eagle Books, 2025

**A POET'S PROMISE**
by **Rositta Joseph**

Copyright © Rositta Joseph

All rights reserved. No part of this publication may be reproduced, stored in a retrieval system, or transmitted, in any form or by any means, electronic, mechanical, photocopying, recording or otherwise without the prior permission of the publisher.

Cover Photograph and Design: **Dr Georgitta Joseph Valiyamattam**
Interior Design: Ezy's Publication

ISBN- 978-1-64560-662-8 (Paperback)
Library of Congress Control Number: 2025933749

Printed in the United States of America

*For my Daddy*
*Mr. Joseph Valiyamattam*
*who first believed in my poems,*

*for Gitanjali Ghei (1961-1977)*
*whose verses conquered death,*

*and*

*for Jayanta Mahapatra (1928-2023)*
*who made me feel, like never before,*
*the power of poetry.*

*The desire of the moth for the star,*
*Of the night for the morrow,*
*The devotion to something afar*
*From the sphere of our sorrow?*

> 'To..' by Percy Bysshe Shelley

*To strive, to seek, to find, and not to yield.*

> 'Ulysses' by Alfred Lord Tennyson

# Foreword

## Meher Pestonji

In an age of instant gratification where internet offers immediate publication on poetry sites and poets are challenged to write a poem a day, Rositta Joseph has chosen to stand apart by publishing her first collection of poetry after thirty years, revealing a rare maturity.

It's worth the wait, for we see the trajectory of her growth from an idealistic adolescent

> Racing against
> That undefeated tyrant
> Called time ('A Poet's Promise')

to the mature woman

> Dancing gracefully
> Without protest
> With a smile
> On the tightrope
> Between
> Love and Hate
> Laughter and Tears

> Selflessness and Selfishness
> Hope and Despair ('A Fine Balance').

Yes, the journey to maturity is a long meander with triumphs and challenges.

I'm privileged to have observed Rositta's growth from her doctoral thesis on the role of literature in rewriting national history from the margins to her flowering into a passionate literature professor. Teaching is central to her life, enabling her to go

> Riding on the crests of the tallest minds
> Diving into the depths of the deepest souls
> ('For the Love of Literature').

Drawing on her literary explorations, she crafts poetry imbued with philosophical wisdom yet as contemporary as her students:

> We found a soulmate in AI
> And a philosopher in ChatGPT.
> The Truth has died
> Laughing at
> The heights
> We have reached ('Post Truth').

The young Rositta celebrates falling in love. For her, love is not a conventional giving over of body and soul to the loved one. She categorically states,

> I had very clear ideas about space,
> Until
> You intruded into
> My well-guarded queendom.
> And ever so stealthily,
> Made it your own ('Space').

Fiercely guarding independence, she describes her fiercely feminist relationship in an amazingly honest voice.

I am the one
You think you know
But you never really know.
Not appealing, but powerful
Not soothing, but meaningful.
I have swallowed
All your darkness
Borne all your pain.

Look at me, man,
I am your
Ego-crushing truth
Soul-searing solace
I have let you win,
You cannot bear loss
I have glorified my sorrow,
You can never bear
The pain you inflict ('Deep Brown Ocean').
This is tenderness camouflaged in soul strength.

Travelling, another passion, takes Rositta to many cities from Hyderabad to Ahmedabad as well as to jungles. From Tirumala, she hears about a tiger killing a five-year-old child with predictable reactions from villagers and officials while the bereaved parents sit with heads bowed. Discarding fake sympathy she views the situation with candid pragmaticism:

No one sees
The gleaming truth
Of one tender tiger,
Divinely ordained
To end in
The swift and

> Soft jungle way
> A tiny life destined for
> Endless misery
> In the inhuman
> Company of
> Human beings ('Tiger At Tirumala').

Travel also takes her to pilgrimage places questioning physicality with childish rebellion. She enters the Tanjore temple asking,
> Why should fort after fort,
> Wall after wall,
> Protect an old temple? ('The Temple At Tanjore').

Soon the spiritual ambience seeps into her being and she confesses,
> Questions enter first,
> Dragging me after.
> Stunned by the enormity
> Of what I almost missed,
> Consciousness freezes
> Into time travel and
> A desperate
> Struggle for words...
> How do you paint paradise
> Or communicate the cosmos?
> ('The Temple At Tanjore').

Taking nothing for granted, Rositta remains open to questioning her own preconceptions. That's what makes her a great teacher and mentor. And her poems, gems of eternal value.

# Critical Introduction

## A Poet's Courage as the Promise to Fight for Right(s)

## Arjuna Parakrama

Rositta Joseph's is a poetry of commitment, the strident voice of her social conscience writ large, and yet she has accomplished this through a humility and self-deprecation that conveys her social critique without being judgmental of us her readers, nor, indeed, of the general public, though she spares no one who abuses privilege or power. Her overarching theme and concern is the outcome of injustice, suffering and exploitation, in relation to which her focus remains public and altruistic, even when it is deeply personal, as she writes

> Yet, my tears fall
> For other broken hearts
> And myriad desperate voices
> Piercing the skies. . . .
>
> Compassion is your gift to me,
> Mother. ('Velankanni')

This "gift" of compassion is always concrete and

specific, never vague or platitudinous, as she seeks to better understand sociopolitical problems and more fully engage with core concerns of inequality, so that she may catalyse change that is systemic. Her poetic task is to unmask the bedrock injustice that pre-determines the future of the "toiling peasant child", following in the footsteps of her parents, so that we may work to change, meaningfully and sustainably what Joseph despairingly describes as the inescapable sorrow that lies in wait.

> Shall I speak of three ages in one age?
> Three nations in one?
> Or three worlds in one world? [. . .]
>
> The toiling peasant's child
> Will sit on mud floors
> Begin learning what the rest of the world has finished
> Just enough to toil like enslaved
> fathers and mothers [...]
>
> One equaliser for all
> Innocence at the beginning
> Sorrow at the end
> Always Inescapable. ('Equaliser')

Hence, her rejection of the structural and epistemic brutality of our times is trenchant and unequivocal. In an epoch where "third world" poetry is turning inward in troublingly self-indulgent and depoliticized ways, Joseph's voice resonates a radically different perspective. In this next example, her scathing critique of elite hypocrisy uses a conventional image of the mask but with a powerful twist that awakens us to the fact that these masks become the person hiding inside, disfiguring and dehumanizing them as captured in the pain-invoking image of stitching flesh, made more troubling by the deliberate blurring of the us/them distinction. Is there no difference then between the elites as drivers of injustice and us as those who accept and confirm to it, when truth is the real casualty?

> Permanent actors
> With masks
> Stitched to our souls. [. . . ]
>
> The Truth has died
> Laughing at
> The heights
> We have reached. ('Post Truth')

Yet, it is simplistic to see her understanding of the magnitude of the forces arrayed against justice as always being able to prevail over the ethical. While it is true that at moments in the poetry, as seen in the lines quoted above, Joseph feels lost and despairing, at other times her courage and conviction come through equally strongly on the side of the angels of hope:

> All is never lost
> For
> Those who walk
> The straight and narrow path
> In a crooked world. ('Return to School')

"All is never lost" and thus her impatience with all kinds of hypocrisy and self-seeking rationalizations is as refreshing as it is insightful. Joseph's poetry is not of the kind that comes from privilege or dalliance. In the words of another poet, she has "paid its price", as she asserts, [I]

> Have neither the time nor the money
> For the 'right' kind of holidays,
> Have lived in a hurry
> From one futile struggle to another – ('Rebel').

The fact that she can calmly and matter-of-factly confirm "I know the limits of my time and my purse" ('Rebel') raises the value and opportunity cost of her writing beyond self-indulgence and classist fashion. Her life is characterised by the "hurry" imposed by the bombardment of issues and catastrophes demanding her undivided attention.

Rositta Joseph's poetic courage is infectious, all the more so because it is far from being dogmatic or propagandist, and hence simplistic. Her range includes deeply personal poems, which acknowledge and celebrate the core influences in shaping her thought and action. Especially moving is her tribute to her father for empowering and nurturing her growth. In terms of poetic skill, note the daring use of the single line occupied by "To" which dangles tantalizingly, creating both doubt and expectation, that fittingly culminates in the juxtaposition of the infinite (the universe) with the most mundanely concrete (the ground under her feet).

> Of a most charming man,
> Who alone possesses the power
> To
> Put the universe
> Under my feet. ('Father's Day')

Joseph demonstrates a rare skill in being able to articulate hidden political truths where others only see the stark beauty of nature, while at the same time opening up this natural space for wonder and enjoyment. The poem 'Kaveri' provides such an example of this skill.

> Kaveri, do we know each other
> From a previous birth? [. . . ]

> They try to claim you
> Both religion and tradition
> But Kaveri, you free spirit,
> As the ancient tribals
> Of your Coorgi forests
> You belong to no one.
> Dipping my fingers
> In your soul- cooling water [. . . ]

> How many Chola champions
> Have suckled on your breasts;
> In your waters they baptized
> Their endless empire
> Of Thanjavur and Trichy.

The fraught complicity between exploitation of people and the manipulation of nature is subtly but surely expressed here, as compounded through the political and ideological use of tradition, culture and religion to serve the interests of power. And yet the river flows on, its "soul-cooling water" shared across all divides and differences, its "free spirit" uncontaminated.

In the poem 'The Temple at Tanjore', deceptively simple questions strike at the heart of the nexus between institutionalised religion and the entrenchment of political power for personal gain.

> Why should fort after fort,
> Wall after wall,
> Protect an old temple?
> Questions enter first,
> Dragging me after. [. . .]
>
> This ode to
> Enormity and symmetry?

This realisation has led the poet to reject conventional belief and its rituals, but not spirituality itself.

> My idols have crumbled,
> My ideals shaken,
> My heart broken,
> I look down at icons that tumbled. [. . .]
>
> To live in a world at war with itself [.]
> ('Innocence At Eighteen')

This reflects the views of the poetic persona at eighteen, which becomes further refined and larger-than-personal, identifying the bigger picture.

> Worship becomes woe
> Faith turns fanatic
> Religion looks revolting. [. . .]
>
> Then, just one prayer
> To be

> Religionless
> Stateless
> And
> Godless. ('Just One Prayer')

These lines are as forceful as they are courageous, coming from both the heart and the head, from someone who has lived this pain. Many will think this but few dare to say it out loud, and hardly anyone with this poetic power that yet retains real anguish.

One of the most important and unique characteristics of Joseph's poetry is her ability to nuance and delineate socioeconomic class, situating herself within her critique of classed values and norms, as seen in 'Middle-Class Indian Memories'.

[. . .]

> Endless love affairs with libraries
> Western fairy tales and Eastern folk tales [. . .]
>
> First job, first book
> First dreams and first promises
> To change the world [. . .]
>
> Sly memory
> Brings me a silk saree or a story book
> A picture I drew or a look
> From loving eyes
> A coffee or a cake or fresh lemon juice from mother's hands
> The scent of rain drops on dry earth
> Teacher father's smile reflected on my students' faces
> Sister's sister talk,

> Lover's laughter
> And I forget everything
> Except for the memory of
> Pure joy.

The middle-class here is marked by its self-absorption and aggrandisement. Yet, the challenge is to remain aloof and unmoved from the gentle critique of our classed preoccupation with books in libraries on the one hand, and the (false) dichotomy between westernization and nativization, or more realistically the crazy mix we have all inhabited in our childhood. Then, there is for her "no greater peace /Than to come home."

One cannot but help noting the shift from the naively impractical idealism of youth (first job, first book ... to change the world), which is again a function of this aggrandisement of the middle class as change agents for the underclass, and hence not innocent. This movement then leads to the soft and lyrical section with which the poem ends by invoking the cherished moments of middle-class life, at once ordinary and special, trivial and momentous, small and large. The love and protection of family is beautifully captured in a few poignant images, exquisitely wrought to invoke the feelings that transcend narrow class boundaries but are still firmly rooted in the middle-class milieu. To universalize these is the trap that Joseph refuses to embrace, situating them in her past as their essence and not their trappings.

It is because of her hard-won awareness that Joseph is able to recognise that this life and its values are also limiting, even misleading if one wants to see the larger picture and to intervene in the bigger battles. In 'Memories', a haunting poem that both embraces and fights nostalgia, in the wake of the COVID-19 pandemic, she writes

> We live in the past,
> The present seems dead,
> The future is too fragile,
> Vanishing before we visualise.
> From the faint lingering warmth
> of ancient embraces,
> Out of the fading imprints
> of old sight-seeing journeys,
> Over the scanty fragrance of
> the free breaths we took aeons ago,
> We fight to live. [. . . ]
>
> Prisoners in our own houses,
> Separated from most of what we cherish,
> We cling on to the feather
> That can give us new life -
> Memories.

In the last lines, the poem pushes beyond the immediate confines of its pandemic context to encapsulate a broad principle of contemporary life, unable to resist or contest the tragic developments of our times, be they at home or abroad. Ours is a generation marked by the normalization of violence, the fetishization of disparity. Joseph is only too aware of

> Wrong choices to stay back in wrong places
> In a wrong land, with wrong people[.]
> ('Return to School')

Yet, ultimately, the poems and the poet are irrepressible. Like 'Lakshmi Bai' and the heroines in 'The Phoenixes of Bombay', Joseph is "A heart / Embracing the universe." She recognises the fragility of this moment, the hugeness of the task ahead of her, the disappointments that are inevitable:

> I have fallen from the sky
> A hundred times;
> Surviving
> Only because
> Someone
> Had softly spread
> My dreams
> On the ground. ('A Fine Balance')

Her solution is to think globally, to envision planetarily, and still to remain firmly rooted to the earth and its people. Poetry is an avocation, not a pastime, wherein she asks rhetorically,

> Is writing one poem per day
> Enough to fool yourself? ('Waiting to be Refuted')

Instead, Joseph demands of herself and the world to

> Give me wings
> Make me a child
> That I may give to each
> In body, mind,
> Heart and soul. ('Two Worlds')

These poems share with us the poet's special wings

that allow her to survey the universe of her values, yet to see through the eyes of a child as if for the first time, while at the same moment to plant the seeds of her dreams on the ground, so that all who wish may hear.

# Poet's Note

## Rositta Joseph

A poem is deeply personal and undeniably universal at the same time. It is this magical quality of poetry that has given me the confidence to share my inmost feelings with all of you. I fervently hope that these feelings will be understood and echoed in a myriad ways.

My first poem came at the age of ten or eleven, when I had my first glimpse of the magnificent Arabian Sea from the southwestern coast of India. It was a one-liner that went like this: "As the waves of the sea cover the sand, again and again, winning a victory, so shall I win a victory over evil…" It was a child's expression of awe at Nature's power and glory interspersed with the value system she had been exposed to. Though I had no knowledge of similes and metaphors, and extremely childish though the attempt was, my father's unbounded enthusiasm in appreciating my outburst meant the world to me. Then began the adventure of adding poems to my diary whenever something or someone touched my small world, followed by the unconditional admiration of my parents and sometimes embarrassing poetry readings before guests and friends and relatives.

However, the spark was firmly lit and did not die out despite all the challenges life threw at me, testing my faith and hope and self-belief. As I grew out of childhood, poetry writing continued, but no longer for other ears. It was more of a private ritual that was meant to affirm my faith in my own abilities and to help me deal with life in a more positive manner. It was the struggle to release volcanic, cyclonic emotions and to stand apart from the crowd. Despite the lack of self-confidence that kept these poems unpublished for close to three decades now, I did nurture a secret dream that one day these poems would see the light of day and be welcomed to formally merge themselves with the larger ocean of human thought and feeling.

So, as I humbly place a piece of my heart and mind and soul before the readers, I wish to reiterate the simplicity of my poems. Despite my encounters with literature and literary theories, canonical poetry and varied schools of poets, the innocent child who first wrote those simple lines inspired by the ocean dominates my work. Yes, these poems are emotions recollected in tranquillity; they are a letting loose of emotion and a distancing from emotion; they are a reflection of my personality and a running away from the self; they are a means to escape into an imaginary and better world; they are also weapons to face the challenges of life. While some of them are allies for hard times, others just reflect the bitter truths of life.

The sixty-three poems gleaned from close to three decades of writing are arranged into different sections. These sections are ordered in the manner in which my life has evolved over the years: from poetry as an innocent pleasure to a passion. This collection begins with the love for Nature that inspired my first poems, moving on to my encounters with varied human relationships and emotions, to the spirituality that has often been tested but emerged as a strong rock amid all the turbulence of life, to the unquenchable thirst for literature as a student and teacher, the quest for and finding of true love, the experiences gained from fond memories of travel and exploration across the country and beyond, the reflections upon the myriad contemporary worlds we inhabit, the assertion of womanhood in its pain and glory, and finally the section titled 'Survival' wherein poetry becomes both a record and a means of battling all odds.

Nevertheless, all the poems are bound together by one thread – 'A Poet's Promise'. As promised in the first two poems in this collection, every poem is an offering of love to the readers. These poems embody existence, identity, struggle, survival, and above all, raw humanity. Through moments of despair and elation, light and darkness, they have been my catharsis, inspiration and undying hope.

Poetry is born, I believe, when experience exceeds words, and words find fulfilment in serving as mere pointers and maps guiding us to a treasure trove of human emotions. Each of us explore and live these emotions in our own ways. I am grateful for this privilege of sharing my journey with you, a journey we can enjoy both individually and together, for it is finally 'our' journey.

# Acknowledgements

This opportunity to be able to finally share my poems with fellow human beings across the world is nothing short of a miracle, for which I am immensely grateful to the Almighty. I shall forever be indebted to my mother Mrs Elsy Joseph who taught me the language, to my father Mr Joseph Valiyamattam who made me realise that my ultimate calling lay in literature, to my sister Dr Georgitta Valiyamattam who patiently became the sympathetic audience, the humorous critic and the sharp editor during long poetry-reading sessions and also designed the book cover, and in a very special way to my husband Mr Anjo K Mathew who tells me during the darkest moments that destruction should never bother me for I am born to create.

Over these years, scores of dedicated teachers, talented students and inspiring colleagues have motivated me to keep writing poetry. The poets I have read, studied and admired, ancient and modern, young and old, from every part of the globe, have played a key role in keeping my small lamp burning all through. Above all, I am deeply thankful to life itself, to Nature, to the varied experiences and places and persons I have come across. Every single day has shaped my poems.

I am forever grateful to Ms Meher Pestonji, journalist, social activist, dramatist, poet and novelist. Her fiery writing and relentless social service have inspired me for close to a decade now. She has always been an unfailing source of guidance during my doctoral studies, my post-doctoral project and now in the publication of my first volume of poetry. It is my honour and privilege that she has written the Foreword to this book.

Professor Arjuna Parakrama, globally renowned human rights activist, author, poet and former professor of literature at Colombo and Peradeniya universities is someone I literally adore. His unwavering commitment to defending the rights of the voiceless amid the harshest conditions is unparalleled for its raw courage and devotion to the truth. Thank you so much, Arjuna, for finding time to write a detailed and exceptional critical introduction for this volume of poetry. It means the world and beyond to me and will always be one of the proudest moments of my life.

The most special note of thanks will always be for Dr Basudhara Roy, an eminent poet and passionate teacher, the angel who has held my hands and guided me. She has been a most generous mentor and her faith in my poetry is priceless. The note she has written for this book will always have a special place in my heart, and so will Dr Umesh Kumar, a dear friend, noted scholar and faculty at Benares Hindu University, who introduced me to Basudhara.

Dr Sangeetha Puthiyedath, an exceptionally gifted author and faculty at EFLU, Hyderabad has been very kind in analysing my poems using her keen academic lens. I am deeply obliged to this beloved and affectionate teacher of mine, her for her time and effort.

Finally, I am immensely grateful to Mr Satya Pattanaik and his team at Black Eagle Books, USA. Their selfless commitment to the cause of promoting Indian writing globally is highly praiseworthy. I have really loved every moment of this publication journey with their warm and professional team.

- **Rositta Joseph**

# Contents

| | |
|---|---|
| Foreword | ix |
| Critical Introduction | xiii |
| Poet's Note | xxiv |
| Acknowledgements | xxvii |

### A Poet's Promise
- A Poet's Promise — 1
- Rebel — 2

### Nature
- Dusk — 4
- The Unkindest Cut — 5
- Animals, Humans — 6
- The Curse of Hussain Sagar — 7

### Relationships
- Father's Day — 10
- Eros — 12

### Emotions
- Courage — 19
- Sacrifice — 20

### Spirituality
- Faith Anthem — 21
- Will He Come? — 22
- The Legend of Saint George — 26

**For the Love of Literature**
- To Teach a Literature Class    28
- In Our Literature Classes    30

**Love**
- Alone Together    35
- Betrayal    36
- Change    38
- Space    42
- When We Meet Next    43
- Litany in Honour of Love    44

**Places**
- Adalaj    46
- Ahmedabad    48
- Araku    50
- Chowmahalla Palace    51
- City of Destiny    53
- Highway Chronicles    55
- Kaveri    57
- Moonlight Sonata    62
- Take Me Back    64
- The Peace of Puri    65
- The Temple at Tanjore    67
- Velankanni    75

**The World**
- Avatar    78
- Equaliser    80
- Innocence at Eighteen    82
- Just One Prayer    86
- Manipur    87
- Memories    89

- Middle-Class Indian Memories  90
- Moon Song  93
- Post Truth  95
- Spy Versus Soldier  96
- Tiger at Tirumala  99
- Two Worlds  101
- Unfair  103
- Waiting to be Refuted  104

## Woman
- Shackles  105
- Deep Brown Ocean  106
- The Disrobing of Draupadi  108
- Lakshmi Bai  114
- The Phoenixes of Bombay  117

## Survival
- A Fine Balance  118
- Evasion  119
- How Easy  121
- Lent to Lent  122
- Long Drive  125
- No Greater Peace  126
- Of Not Making It  128
- Return to School  129
- Shattered  131
- That Whereby Men Live  132

# A Poet's Promise

One painful line at a time
Carved in bitterness
Polished with tears,
Heavy with
The unweighable weight
Of defeat,
Bruised and bled
By the sharpest dagger
Of ruthless criticism,
Racing against
That undefeated tyrant
Called time.

Yet fighting,
Yet lighting,
One tiny lamp
For the cold darkness
Of pure despair.

Let me depart birthing these lines,
If only you would cradle them
Do not let them fade…
Raw, crazed,
They will return your love
A thousand-fold.
That's a poet's promise.

# Rebel

I do not claim the right or the luxury
To write well-crafted poetry.
I was not educated at the 'right' places
Nor did I rub shoulders with the 'right' poets
Blessed by the 'right' mentors
And 'right' publishers.
I have been 'wrong' all my life.
And proud of it.
I know of writing retreats
And writing breaks
In the mountains and
On the seashores,
Have neither the time nor the money
For the 'right' kind of holidays,
Have lived in a hurry
From one futile struggle to another -
Bread and butter,
Worries and cares,
Criticism and soul-crushing work,
Ingratitude and betrayal,
And after all this -
A sense of utter worthlessness.
This is where I come from.
Have rushed through mountains and rivers
Glanced hungrily at fabulous cities and villages

Run through castles and palaces,
Churches and temples -
I know the limits of my time and my purse,
So, I swallow all that I sense,
Gorge greedily on every moment.
May not digest everything,
But, in between teaching
And cooking dinners
Working online, offline, overtime
And doing the dishes
And being looked down upon
For the sin of being born feminine,
Some of what I have experienced
And seen and loved and feared
Will become part of my blood,
And re-appear as the words in my 'wrong' poems
Perhaps ignored by the 'right' scholars
But certainly smelling of the untameable pride
Of 'wrong' and 'wronged' women.

*Nature*

## Dusk

Weariness travels
Towards nests and homes
Light fades
Coolness cascades
Skies set on fire
Blue to orange to gray
Clouds change their attire
To mark the burning of day
Dusk arrives in glory
Carrying moon and stars
And many a bedtime story.

## The Unkindest Cut

There lies the tree,
That
Stood by my window once
So proud and so free.
There it lies,
Embracing the earth that nurtured it,
Staring at the sun that strengthened it,
Lamented by the breeze that caressed it.
Did not fall,
Had to be felled.
Not an easy job,
Deep roots wrenched out
Hefty boughs chopped up
Ancient bark stabbed upon,
Repeatedly.
Still, not enough.
The most unkindest cut
Of
Ingratitude
And
Betrayal.
And then,
The end.

## Animals, Humans

The humanity of animals is infinite
Just like the bestiality of humans
The stray cat protecting
Her fragile kittens
All alone
On a freezing dark
Rainy night
Outside our big warm
Cosy house.

## The Curse of Hussain Sagar

A Nizam dreamt of water
For his parched people;
And his terrified minister
Turned a fake treasure hunt
Into real lake-building.

Aeons ago
Deeps of heaven
Deeps of earth
Were conjured
To burst forth,
Flooding
The core of
This ancient city.

Now, glowing gardens and pleasure parks
A behemoth Buddha:
Rugged rock amid vast voluptuous waters,
Musical fountains,
Dancing feasts on floating ships;
I rode the dizzying deep on a moonlit night
Sailboat and speedboat
Backdropped by glittering Necklace Road.

Just ahead in a hi-tech palace,
Beside ancient Nizami monuments
Behind the largest Ambedkar monolith
And a gleaming memorial to Telangana's martyrs
Sit their proudly unworthy successors,
Legislating and ruling.

Despite every effort
Bitter truth cannot be forgot
Man-made, glittery night
Can't hide the
Inky blackness and foul stench
Of waste and sewage
From an ungrateful city.

Offering undeserved pleasure
Amid unbearable pain
The lake growls menacingly
At hordes of callous polluters
Merciless murderers
Of Nature's magnificence.

Next to me, on the rocking boat,
Cameras in hand,
My companion hears explosions,
Sees blood and corpses,
Time travelling decades ago,
To some serial blasts,
On these very banks;
And I wonder,
Is it Hussain Sagar's curse?

Women and men in uniform,
Builders and artists,
Environmentalists
Fighting back
For a secure, man-made paradise;
Failing to hide the ugly unkindness
Of humans to Hussain Sagar?

Abusers of history's treasures
Butchers of nature's bounty
It will haunt you,
Hyderabad –
The curse of Hussain Sagar!

*(Note: Hussain Sagar is the largest lake in Hyderabad, built by the Nizams.)*

*Relationships*

## Father's Day

We disagree often
And
Talk rarely.
Living on separate planes
in selfish cocoons
Of ambitious busy youth
And complaining sceptical
Old age.
Strangely though,
We are a team.
No words, no expressions
Memory alone suffices
For undisputable understanding
Of each other's virtues and villainy.
Long years have made
Deep gulfs -
Handiwork of folly, vice, destiny.
But just one moment,
All cliffs crumble,
And I time travel,
Daddy's little girl -

Cuddling in the strongest arms
Of a most charming man,
Who alone possesses the power
To
Put the universe
Under my feet.

# Eros*

Yesterday,
On the beach,
I saw, two kids
Walk hand in hand;
I remembered you,
My friend.

Shared times
Long lazy afternoons
Exciting trips
To nowhere
Endless small talk
And forbidden gossip.

Birthdays, feast days,
Letters and handmade cards,
Preserved for years
Like differences of opinion.

Too much of togetherness
Ripening into irritation and
Bursting out as teary arguments.
Yet, a few hours apart,
And the longing to hear
Each other's voices.

Strange, we often talked
Philosophy
And trusted our instincts,
Had sharp sixth senses
Yet could never sense the enemy within.

With time
We grew apart.
I feared your religiosity
And You, my worldliness.

Too many pressing demands.
Replying to letters,
Even answering your telephone calls
Became a chore.

Somewhere,
We became strangers.
But the bonds were too strong
And pulled us together again.

Surprisingly,
Even our combined wisdom
Could not decipher
That we were surviving
On borrowed time.

Your little aches and fevers
And that fashionable cough,
For which you made me buy
Self-prescribed medicines
Irritated me no end.
I never knew
The days were numbered.

So much so
That when the doctors
Gave their verdict
And pronounced
The dreaded
Six-letter word

It felt like a
Sledgehammer
Slowly pounding
The mind to a pulp.
For only yesterday,
You were skipping in the rain,
While I watched from
The safety of my umbrella.

But you,
You took the news too well.
For you,
The chemo,
The medicines that induced nausea,
The injections that left you
Writhing for hours
And, your lustrous locks falling
Faster than autumn leaves
Were a sure means to
Attain paradise.

But me,
Worldly me,
What was I to do?
First, the anger
That you kept your illness

To yourself
And watered the
Poison plant within,
Drove me almost
Insane.

Then,
The hoping against hope.
The fervent prayers,
Offerings at every altar,
The failed attempts at austerity,
The vows made
To light candles, go on
Pilgrimages, give alms
If you left your hospital bed.

Still, even the momentary
Sense of well-being
Was a deception.
The physician claimed,
No toxic cell remained.
But all the while,
Fate was mocking us.
And the reddish glow on
Your ruddy cheeks
Was only the last flicker
Of a dying flame.

Clasping at fleeing hope,
When you were again shifted
To the hospital.
Admire your skills,
Your well-planned routine,

The way you worried
For the lady in the next cubicle,
Till her corpse left,
And you accepted all.

Later,
When they covered you
With drips, tubes, masks
And the emotionless nurse
Suctioned your blistered throat
As you drifted in and out
Of consciousness
I checked your bag
And found it empty.
You cheat!
You had given away all your
Titbits as gifts to me,
You knew it all.

Gradually,
I grew a death wish
For You.
How could I get used to
Seeing unfeeling strangers
Handle you all day,
You, so proud,
So independent,
Now small and vulnerable
Against the white linen.

Yes, call me 'selfish',
'cowardly'.
I began to fear your room -

For I could smell Death
In disinfectants
And hear It in beeping machines.
I wanted to Live.
 - EROS.

Here,
Here we had to part ways,
This far, No further.
This was your tryst,
Not mine.
You were a painful memory.
One deathly silent afternoon,
When your labored breathing
Struck terror into my heart,
I told you,
It's alright to go.
The moment
I turned my back,
You were gone.
You had the last laugh.

Had to keep up appearances
At your funeral,
For my tears had
Dried up long ago.
But, took care to
Dress carefully,
For you were so proud of me,
So particular,
And would have wanted to show me off
To everyone.
Did I dare offend you?

You did look lovely, immaculate,
As they lowered you
And I kept wondering
You seemed so at home
Even Down Under.

Just wanted to get over
All the sticky sentiments,
To wipe the slate clean.
Life had enough
Didn't need one more pain.
So, I consciously erased
All traces of you.

Yet, when my dog
Barked at space
I wondered if it was You.

Could I erase
The sunlight, starry night
Roses, sea-surf
Soothing breeze
Smiles on children's faces –
Wherever I looked,
I found You,
Unwilling to Go,
Stubborn as ever.
   - EROS again.


( * In Freudian theory, Eros refers to the life-instinct in human beings.)

*Emotions*

## Courage

Reclaiming soul splendour,
Scaring fear away,
Hurting pain.
Unarmed mad men
Beginning after the end.
Crazed women
Diving for a drop of truth
Into falsehood's ruthless ocean.
Choosing a million lives
On one last day
Over
A million deaths
On ten thousand nights.

## Sacrifice

To shun the sweetest of desires
And become bosom friend to betrayal.
Light embracing darkness
Love clinging to hate.
Strength of slaves, mother of mothers,
Ecstasy of rebels, nectar of warriors
Fragrance of no-man's lands.
Fury beyond fury,
No greater charm.
Life-breath of religion,
Soul of spirituality.
Turning every cross to a triumphant sign
Taking mortals beyond the divine.

*Spirituality*

## Faith Anthem

My soul sings for you a song
My heart to you does belong.
Beloved,
My love for you, a limpid fountain
My trust in you, a mighty mountain.
Behold,
As evening shadows draw near
Is it you, calming every fear?
I hear your laughter in the gurgling streams
And see you smile in guileless dreams.
Hide not from my seeking eyes,
Come, be with me, all through
What life without you?
You potter, me clay
Come once, give solace
I pray.
Having glimpsed you,
I stand apart,
Too pure is your heart.
Your love, calm after storm
Your mercy, a sweet return home.
Lead me, embrace me,
Be my Lord.
One thing I know,
You are my God.

## Will He Come ?

A two-thousand-year-old stable
In Bethlehem.
Stillness and stillness
Amidst all mayhem.
Lost in memories of manger dreams
Again and again, the silence screams
Will He Come?

Humble shepherds and
Humbler flocks,
Time turns to rust and dust;
Each age has its sheep,
In search of a master true an' just.
Will He Come ?

One shining star
To proclaim peace and defy war.
Of those three kings,
Each night sings.
Will He Come ?

Gold, frankincense and myrrh,
We offered with élan
To the King and His mother;
He was God and Man.

O, when He smiled,
God's only child.
Will He Come ?

To Egypt we must flee,
Herod's killing spree.
A million voices rend the sky,
Listen, the slaughtered innocent cry.
The path is long forlorn
A colt still waits all alone.
Will He Come ?

At Jerusalem's gates,
Scholars and scribes in unison;
Yet victorious the carpenter's son,
His wisdom they couldn't defeat.
His words they couldn't repeat.
Will He Come ?

Many a Cana hath called,
For the first sign;
When the Creator commanded
The water turned to wine.
To our aid,
Will He Come ?

The blind could see
The dumb could speak
Aye, Aye, the deaf could hear.
We are Mary, We are Martha,
Waiting for our Lazarus dear
We are dead, Raise us to life
Will He Come ?

Who, O Who will pass us by ?
Under the old, old Sycamore tree ?
Yon Zacchaeus ever so shy
And, who will set Matthew free?
Will He Come ?

Many a summer we have seen
Parched, scorched and dry.
Hark! The Samaritan's cry
To give her living water clean
Will He Come ?

Humiliated, hurt and trampled upon
Silenced unto death –
Once a man made a whip of cords
Drove out the unjust, all alone.
Suffering now for centuries here
O give voice to the voiceless
Soothe all our fear
Will He Come ?

Lost, wandering, lifeless
Without a leader
Without a guide
A solemn sermon up on the Mount
Five thousand fed from love's eternal fount
O, for us His deep, deep passion
Desire we that compassion
Will He Come ?

Knowledge there is too much
And scholars too many;
But we understand only

Some parables as such.
Could you tell us any
As the Nazarene used to?
Will He Come ?

Unmatched glory,
Peerless grandeur-
This wide, wondrous world has shown,
Yet, time stood still at Tabor alone
Will He Come ?

Every cross beckons,
Every supper reminds,
Every garden looks like Gethsemane.
Only He could wash sinful feet,
Break His body, shed His blood,
 Such Love, O Lord and God,
Love, we thirst for love,
Who can refuse, who can reject ?
Will He Come ?

Judged, scourged,
King of the Jews,
Greeted by scorns,
Crowned with thorns-
For us He triumphed on Calvary,
Again in Triumph, will He come.


*(Note: The poem is a rendering of the life of Jesus Christ, chiefly based upon the Holy Bible.)*

## The Legend of Saint George

Middle Eastern warrior-prince
Heart larger than largeness
Courage fiercer
Than fiercest dragons
Protector of the weak
Guardian of the just
Sought by kings and emperors

Until,
His fatal choice of faith over power
That began his divine innings.

'Saint George Strike For Us'
Battle-cry of armies everywhere
Refuge of those stricken
By fear and poison
North of Europe to
Deep south
Of India
Princes and pontiffs
Beyond faiths and creeds
Speak of the phantom horseman
Appearing
Wherever goodness is threatened…

George, Giorgio, GeeVarghese
They love him in every tongue
The brave, demon-slaying, golden-hearted knight.

(*Note: Saint George, a medieval knight, is honoured as a saint by the Catholic and Orthodox churches all over the world.*)

*For the Love of Literature*

## To Teach a Literature Class

All my life
I have burned with the desire to
Know your knowledge
and
Word your wisdom.

O Literature,
How I pursued you
Barefoot,
Only to see you moving
Farther away.

What have I not risked?
Where have I not searched?
Speaking of you to every speck.
Why this endless mirage?

In a world that
Walks over the soul,
I wished only
Your presence.
Homeless and ridiculed
Always enslaved by

Your bewitching prophecy
Your nectar once tasted,
Never forgotten
And one desire alone -
To teach a literature class

Forever and ever
In this life
And the next.

## In Our Literature Classes

How many stars we touched my friends,
And O yes, the ocean deeps we explored!
Flew through galaxies
Danced through forests
Became rivers and winds
Volcanoes and earthquakes
Hurricanes and cyclones
Fire and flood, we turned into.

Burning summer sun-like, in fury, wisdom, pain
Pouring down rain-like, gentle and deluge
Sometimes life-giving, sometimes all-ending.
We, warmth and joy and quiet patience -
Celebrating frozen winter
Befriending snowstorms
Awaiting spring.

Spring buds and birds we always were,
My children!
Full of life and promise,
Beauty and hope,
And the undying music of life,
In our literature classes.

Living the stories we read

Consuming characters
Embodying emotions
Fighting for ideas.

Tagore and Shakespeare
Emerson and Tennyson
Keats and Yeats
Achebe and Anand
Ngugi and Narayan
Toru and Kamala.
Spenser's sweetness, Donne's sharpness, Milton's magnificence
Dryden, Pope, Swift, Orwellian satire unsurpassed
Marlowe and Shelley, passion personified.
Wordsworth the prophet, Keats the artist
Bacon's hammer blows of wisdom
Lamb's silken tugs of nostalgia.
Jane Austen, first queen of innocent romance
Bronte sisters - daughters of fury, sorrow and piercing love.
Burns lost in love's red, red roses
Blake and Gray in the afterlife
Coleridge romancing ghosts
Byron and Shelley tearing tradition apart.
Arnold, ever critical moralist
Browning, optimistic psychologist.
Yeats and Eliot voicing voiceless post-modernity
Owen, Graves, Larkin, Brecht warring war
Beckett, Pinter, Sylvia Plath, Camus
Inhabiting depths of despair
Conrad exposing our deep darkness.
Ibsen, Shaw, Golding and our very own Karnad
Blinding brilliance of ideas

Thomas Hardy fighting our fate
Dickens awakening our dead conscience.
Virginia Woolf and Margaret Atwood
Stunning feminine glory.
Great American song of humanity -
Whitman, Longfellow, Miller, O'Neill,
Hemingway, Fitzgerald, Henry James.
Emily Dickinson, lover of death, philosopher of the tiny
Poe, O'Henry - story-tellers for all times
Langston Hughes, Alice Walker - Afro-American pride
Toni Morrison - priestess of the Black Goddess
Wole Soyinka, African lion in
Gordimer's Afro soul.
Sarojini's nightingale melodies
Ramanujan's acidic satire
Manto and Attia burning in partition sagas
Khushwant's Singh all-encompassing vastness
All kinds of prose -
Gandhi's and Kalam's utility, Aurobindo's spirituality
Radhakrishnan's philosophy, Nehru's and Tharoor's elegance
Vivekananda's and Ambedkar's revolutionary zeal.
Soul's staple food
in Narayan's Malgudi
and Bond's Mussorie.
Women showing women the way –
Sahgal, Desai, Deshpande
Roy and Divakaruni
Ismat Chughtai and Maya Angelou.
Rushdie, Naipaul, Mistry, Ghosh - rebellious

cosmopolitans
O the fire of our vernacular -
Kalidasa to Tagore to Bankim to Pritam
Bharati to Gorakhpuri, Iqbal to Dhasal
Tendulkar to Vijayan and Ananthamurthy
Our fiercely brilliant women - Goswami,
Mahaswetha, Volga.
Whoever loved like Neruda or Rilke or Marquez?
Or spoke suffering like Sophocles or Tolstoy or
Gorky ?
Or rhymed sorrow like Jayanta Mahapatra?
Thoreau, Ruskin, Raja Rao
Arun Joshi, Noam Chomsky
Navigating ethical oceans.
Sartre, Said, Ahmad and Guha,
Spivak and Bhabha, Fanon, Senghor
Grilling the white man, singing the subaltern soul.
Curnow and Hope and Wright –
Great South soul searchers.
Vikramasimha, Naheed, Nasreen,
Dharker, Diop -
Lanka, Pakistan, Africa,
Incurable rebels all,
From Valmiki to Dhasal
Bama and Ao and Dai
Painting the invisible East -
Dalits, Brown Women, Tribes.

We became all of them
And more than them
Daring to dare them.

Riding on the crests of the tallest minds

Diving into the depths of the deepest souls
We marvelled at and tried to be
All that a human could be.

Imagination stopped where we began
Creativity struggled, pacing our racing hearts
Revolution loved us like a crazed lover
We rebelled more than rebellion.

Religion to Faith
Mysticism to Spirituality
We blossomed
Strength to strength
Rising above and beyond,
Universal and sub-atomic.

What could I teach you
My children?
I could only show the path.
You travelled,
Lived, laughed, wept,
Until
You returned
To show me new things
On my old paths,
And new paths
Never ever dreamt of.

And then I knew
I had made,
An eternal mark,
Somewhere,
Upon the universe.

*Love*

## Alone Together

We rode the storm
Danced within the whirlwind
Twirled our ballet into the typhoon
Skipped across the sea storm
And
Stabbed the furies
With our fierce embrace.

Ages ago our souls
Lost each other
Now they collide and dissolve
With the infinite energy
Of pure atoms.

We drink deep
Of dark despair
We do not fear
We have
Become fear.
Alone.
Together.

## Betrayal

There was a happy little fount here,
That sprung without art.
Travellers came from afar and near,
To quench their thirst and depart.

The more they drank,
The more it gave.
Until you played that painful prank,
You sweet thief, dear knave.

After you had your fill,
The water never will
Flow again,
To comfort those in pain.

It dried up when you left,
Leaving all bereft.
This desert will never bloom.
O! What may banish the gloom?

To your black magic,
There must be some antidote,
In vain have they sought.
Hark! Can they hear the murmur of a stream?
Or is it a waking dream?

No, Never, Ever
Will the spring burst forth,
Thus the wise men quoth,
Till His feet touch and make whole,
The parched earth of Her soul.

## Change

Nothing's the same
After you
My love.
No sound sweeter
Than
Your voice.

When I see the sea
I remember only
Our lost-for-words
Ship gazing.

I look at the blue sky
Through both of our eyes
Lying on the grass
Under a mango tree
Heart of a small forest
Summer day
With a sweet breeze
Do you remember?

I see flowers
And look around
To hear
Your camera clicks

I act irritated
But wait for you
To
Make me pose
Don't you know?

Mountains and Rivers
Ask me
Where is your love?
The highways are
Haunted by our old road trips
And those
Yet to be.

Mirrors seem incomplete,
Till your reflection
Stands beside mine.
Perfumes mock me,
When I seek
Your scent.

Cars laugh at me
You know why?
I sit next to the driver's seat
Waiting for your strong pull
And
Deep kiss.

Any food makes me smile
Cos your hands fed me.

Hummed songs, Handlocked couples,
Cosy beds on cold days,

Hotels, heights, buddies, beauties…
Everywhere I feel you.

Rain reminds me
Taxis and rickshaws
Sitting tight inside
Strong squeezes
Stolen kisses
That's heaven, my love.

The taxi drivers you invite for lunch
Ambulance sirens you pray for
Old parents you treat like gods
Children you love to play with
Siblings you care about so much
Small jokes you laugh so hard at
Strangers you embrace as your own…
Everything screams out only your name

Even in churches, no escape…
Where you stand outside to pray
God steps out to say hello…

Sadness, anger,
possessiveness, poetry,
love letters, bikes…
Every day, date,
Month, year, anniversary,
Stayed together or apart,
Gained or lost…
All passionate things
Filled with your name.

When I see babies
Imagine our future daughter
With your slaying smile
When I see old couples
Dream of
Seaside kisses at ninety.

There's no escape
From you my dear
Nor do I want to

There's no I, now, my dear,
I lost myself, long ago,
It's only You!

## Space

I had very clear ideas about space,
Until
You intruded into
My well-guarded queendom.
And ever so stealthily,
Made it your own.
Until I could find no space of mine
That did not contain you.
Now, you, they, all
Tell me to
Give you space.
Too funny.
I can be logical in all things
Restrained in all things
Understanding in all things
But this.
If I agree,
Where do I go?
Man, I gave you
All my space
Long ago.

## When We Meet Next

Now, I must depart
The play's over.
Next time,
We shall meet earlier.

Million moments more
More soul smiles
More perfect peace.

I shall wait for you…
One life's nothing
For our kind of love.

Every end
Just flows
Into another
Beginning…

# Litany in Honour of Love

Bitter honey
Perfect pain
Eagerly awaited suffering
Escape from every despair
Best of all consolations
Worst of all sorrows
Embracing all
Most exclusive
Irony of ironies
Greatest of illusions
Deepest of truths
Honesty in the worst
Deception of the best
Treasured by the poor
Poverty of the rich
Wisdom among fools
Folly of the wise
Maturity in youth
Youth of old age
Endless energy
Ceaseless peace
Melting stone hearts
Freezing fiery minds
Fount of life
Door to death

Making ugly enchanting
And beautiful lifeless
Begets paradise
Lets loose hell
Supreme attribute of the divine
And
Divine attribute of the human.

## Adalaj

In the heart of India's West
Beat tales of an ancient kingdom
Vaghela warrior Rana Veer Singh
Wedded to Rudabai
Beauty beyond compare
Sole mission
Water for her thirsty people
A stepwell built
Halted by a conqueror
Who took her husband's life
Not her goal
Bartered stepwell
In return for herself
So was completed
The Vav of Adalaj
By Sultan Begda
Grander than any palace
An ornate well
To quench the heart's thirst
Of humans, animals, fields and forests
And of Ruda, queen of hearts
Immersed forever
In its deep waters

Body water
Soul immortal
To this day
Adalaj
Worships the queen
That
Loved, lived
Took her life
To quench
Her people's
Thirst.

*(Note: Adalaj Stepwell or Rudabai Stepwell is a five-storey stepwell located in the small town of Adalaj, close to Gandhinagar city in the Indian state of Gujarat. It was built in 1498 in the memory of Rana Veer Singh of the Vaghela dynasty.)*

## Ahmedabad

City of contradictions
Complicated pasts
All who came
Loved you.

Hindu warriors building temple palaces
On cloud-shrouded mountain peaks
Muslim princes decking you
With dream forts and thousand pillar mosques
And on the banks of Sabarmati
Your mother river
The apostle of peace
Birthing a hermitage
Of truth and non-violence
For the entire universe.

I too came to you
Seeking peace and beauty
Finding murderous falsehood
Ugliest violence
Neatly hidden beneath
Newly white-washed houses
Burnt frequently along with their inmates
And brand-new blue tarpaulin sheets
Behind which riot victims, refugees

Labourers spend entire lifetimes
Doomed to die homeless, nameless.

It's been a long journey, Ahmedabad
From celebrating myriad cultures
To making
Religion, race,
Caste, culture
Easy excuses
For eliminating
Each other.

*(Note: Ahmedabad is the most populous and fastest growing city in the state of Gujarat, Western India.)*

# Araku

Betwixt the Indian ocean
And the forested mountains
Of eastern India
Ageless civilizations on misty cliffs
Million-year-old caves
Peak after peak, valley after valley
Bamboo and pine forests
Seas of flowers
Gentle streams, roaring waterfalls
Coffee, spices, honey
And all things good
Steamed in bamboo
By timeless tribal hands
Primitive drums, nature's own beats
Dances that delight the forests
View-points, sunrise treks, starry bonfires
The haunting melody of our pure love
Unfading, unceasing
Never to be forgotten
In this life
Or the next.

(Note: Araku Valley is a hill station and a valley in the Eastern Ghats of Andhra Pradesh, South India. It is known for its coffee plantations, biodiversity, tribal culture and scenic locations.)

## Chowmahalla Palace

Grace upon grace
Stately symmetry
Blinding brilliance.

A Nizam's
Dalliance with opulence
Passion for perfection
Great kingdom, greater city.

Finest Arabian mares
Rolls Royces for pleasure
Galleries covered in ivory
Middle Eastern mystics, European masters
Crystal-gold chandeliers, marble statues
Porcelain from peerless Far East
Weapons of immortal warriors
Still deadly gleaming
Indian silks, gold, pearls
Diamond-studded robes
Worn by real royals
Gardens, fountains,
Endless lattice windows
Throne rooms, banquet halls
Where history lives in grandeur.

After it all
Whisper of a breeze
Jingling of bangles and anklets
Here lived the loveliest women
Treasures of the harem.

Nothing can capture
Beauty or luxury
Or the tears of those
Caged in golden prisons
Bound by pearl chains.

Women made less than women
Less than human, less than living
Souls trapped in
Every window and flower
Beauty embalmed
Within beauty.

What could be more beautiful
Or
More elegantly, gently
Softly, radiantly
Cruel?

*(Note: Chowmahalla Palace or Chowmahallat is the palace of the Nizams of Hyderabad State located in Hyderabad, Telangana, India.)*

## City of Destiny

Vizag, ocean's brink,
Found my life here
How long should I wait
To live it?
If you are an enchantress
Why do you
Send me away?
Why must
The burdens of life
Be greater
Than your beauty?

A hundred virgin beaches
Million glorious sunrises, sunsets
Deepest green mountains, valleys
Caves, waterfalls
Lighthouse gardens, surf-swept parks
Submarine museums
Ancient universities, naval commands
India's victory at sea
Steel mills, ocean aquariums
Million-year caves, tribal paradises
Spice gardens, coffee museums, chocolate factories
City of pure breeze, healing waters
Best dreams and first love.

I am sinking, Vizag
And I trust
You will not ditch me
I have waited long
Where else can I belong?
Call me back
City of my destiny
I have been yours,
Always.

[*Note: Located between the Eastern Ghats and the Bay of Bengal (Indian Ocean), Visakhapatnam or Vizag (on the East Coast of India) is one of the largest cities in Andhra Pradesh, South India.*]

# Highway Chronicles

No heaven like this
Gliding highways
Topless peaks
Bottomless valleys
Blinding green
Driest desert heat
Thundering monsoon
Snow-kissed breezes
River, sea and lake
Farm, orchard and forest.
Endless discoveries
Flora, fauna, humans
All of Nature
All her glory and terror.

Happy couple, rugged motorbike
Delighted twosome, flying car
Food or water
Comfort or pain
Luxury stays
Camping under stars
Nothing matters
Except you, me
And the journey.
Born to fly

From one universe
To another
Holding hands
And steering wheels
On the wings of
Mad, mad love
How could we
Ever stop?

# Kaveri

Kaveri, do we know each other
From a previous birth?
Why do I keep running into
You again and again?
Ancient river of India's southern heart,
Defying definition and description,
None come to you until you call them,
And you go to no one.

Climbing the Brahmagiri mountains too high
In the ecstasy of newly-wedded love
I found your birthplace.
A small, strong fountain
From earth's womb
Rising in freezing
Magical mysterious mist.
From birth,
They try to claim you
Both religion and tradition
But Kaveri, you free spirit,
As the ancient tribals
Of your Coorgi forests
You belong to no one.
Dipping my fingers

In your soul- cooling water
Bowed goodbye to Tal Kaveri...

But we were destined to meet again
In the endless rose fields
Of Srirangapatna
Only your effervescent water
Could have birthed
Such colour and fragrance.

Heady with rose nectar
Rose perfumes and rose sweets,
My feet danced on the temple steps
of Ranganatha Swami
Where Maha Vishnu
Slept in huge granite garb
Amid ageless rock pillars
Emanating timeless divine power,
Terrifying conquerors.
Just behind Ranganatha's abode
I saw you, flowing shyly, slowly
Kaveri -
Calm and clear,
Quenching divine thirst,
Cleansing human sins.

And then I saw your regal might
You,
Old ally of Srirangam's son
And Mysore's tiger
Sultan Tipu trusted you
To flow into his dungeons and torture
Chained British tyrants

On moonless nights
To nurture his summer gardens
Illumine his many-fountained,
 Multi-hued palaces...
The tiger sleeps forever
Peacefully in your bosom
Rocked by the melody of your waves
Having fought the
Good fight till the end
With the clash of his sword echoing in
Britannia's castle museums
Whispering of the
Most-feared warrior.

And then you do
Your damsel dance
Across the million
Beauty spots
Of the Western ghats;
Then, a furious form,
Trying to breach
Mighty Wodeyar dams;
Calming down as fountains
In paradise gardens
Built by Mysuru Wazirs,
Humming a million
Bygone romances
And honey-dripping dreams.

Kaveri, how you cascade
Down to the great
Tamil Land
How many Chola champions

Have suckled on your breasts;
In your waters they baptized
Their endless empire
Of Thanjavur and Trichy.
Palaces,
Where you reflected
Unbearable radiance
Of fairy princesses
Clothed in emerald-pearls
Ageless temples,
Where Mahadeva never tires
Of immersion
in your vibrant waters...

That rush to meet
The million shrines
Of a Mother
Whose compassion
Engulfs the universe -
Mary of Velankanni
Thousands unburden
Searing desires
Under your gaze
Marian tears mingle
With your waters
Mother Cauvery
As children of
Two mothers meet...

And then, one passionate rush
Into the waiting ocean
Of the east
In your end is

Your beginning
Lady
Kindred Kaveri -
Every woman's
Wondrous journey.

*(Note: The Kaveri is one of the major Indian rivers flowing through the states of Karnataka and Tamil Nadu in South India.)*

## Moonlight Sonata

A cool wooden hut
On an Indian summer night
Deep within deciduous forests
Moon as large as
The love overflowing
In our mischievous
Flaming young hearts
Bounces up and down
On cloud-piercing branches
Chill breeze
Carries bear scents, leopard growls
Deer hooves, python rustles
Deep in the jungle, a tiger roars
Hypnotic murmur
Of a hundred streams
Lulls me almost asleep.

But what rest for a new bride
In the arms of her prince?
Outside
Jungle music comes alive
Inside
One rhythm of
Two hearts

Keeps pace with
Nature's eternal melody.

*(Note: memories of a trip to the forests of
Maredumili in the Eastern ghats, Andhra Pradesh,
India.)*

## Take Me Back

All the delights of plying through
Glittering cities,
Eyes and lips gaping
Heart burning
Mind reeling
At worlds we never knew about
And of course could never afford.
Best of food and dress
Pleasure, licit and illicit,
Jewels and shows and books and toys
Villas and palaces.
You will never have enough of this
And if you ever do,
The guilt will kill you.
O, Take me back to
Where the rich become poor
And the poor rich
Mountains and vales and rivers and woods
Beaches and waves and gardens and springs
O the joy, the hope, the elixir
That
No billionaire can fully experience
And every pauper freely drinks of.

## The Peace of Puri

Addicted to adventure
Lighted by young love
I arrived at Puri.

Home of the one
Who needs no home
Jagannath universal lord
Dwells here
In a ten-thousand-year-old rock
Reaching from earth's womb
To paradise pinnacle.

A sleepless city rushes to meet
The god without eyelids
Amid midnight and dawn.

Outside
Human agents
Promise paradise
For a price.
Far within
The ancient rock
Cool granite floors
Softened to silk
By thousands of peace-seeking feet

Amid the chants of those
Who have given up all
Except Jagannath
You will find
The peace.

That comes from
Renouncing
The universe
And embracing
Its master.

*(Note: Puri, a pilgrim city in Odisha, Eastern India, is famous for the temple of Lord Jagannath.)*

# The Temple at Tanjore

Turning the corner
In the nonchalance
Of an ordinary street,
My tired, reluctant feet
Accidentally step into
Infinity.

Why should fort after fort,
Wall after wall,
Protect an old temple?
Questions enter first,
Dragging me after.

Stunned by the enormity
Of what I almost missed,
Consciousness freezes
Into time travel and
A desperate
Struggle for words...
How do you paint paradise
Or communicate the cosmos?

Thousand and eleven years ago
Raja Raja the first
King of kings

Pride of Cholas
Lord of lands and seas,
Dared his passion
For timeless
Shiva, God of gods -
Making Brihadisvara,
Infinite Vastness Itself,
Dwell within
Marvellous Human Rock.

Where should one begin?
With the creator or the creation
The king or the temple
Where mortals sought
To enshrine Immortality?

Raja Raja Chola
Brave stoic
Detached glory
Father figure, Ruthless invader
Son of the Kaveri, Indian ocean child,
Builder of dams, tamer of tribes,
Lord of endless rice fields
Emerald encrusted cities
Refuge of peasants and merchants,
Patron of warriors and scholars
Terrifying conqueror
Sailing on the seas forever
Bringing the world's treasures
To adorn the feet of his beloved:
Shiva the destroyer.

What whisper you
Ancient rock pavements?
What dream you
Granite pillar giants
With cloud-caressed heads?
Of an emperor who dared to create
Heaven on earth?
Of countless forgotten
Builders, sages, scholars
Who perfected
A passionate monarch's vision?

Domes and arches, towers, spires,
Gopuras, vimanas, shikharas
What tales of love and hate,
Courage, cunning, victory and defeat?
Do you remember
Bull, horse, human, elephant armies
Fetching marble mountains
And rock oceans
For
This ode to
Enormity and symmetry?

Marbled layers
Of Shiva's soul and body
Rocks glued by space
Perfect frescoes –
Radiant blues, reds, whites
Nature's peerless colours.
Fortified by myriad earthquakes
Greater rock than Giza's pyramids
Vaster than vastness

Dream of sculptors and painters -
Demigods who imprisoned
Three worlds in stone:
Angels, demons, gods,
Fairies, warriors, mystics...

What stone inscriptions?
Narrating dreams, drawings,
Definitions of eternity
Prophecies, mysteries,
Magic spells, mystic chants
Mute memorials to
Those who built these
Gates to timelessness.

Narrating labourers, carvers,
Water bearers, stone crushers,
Women and men,
Farmers and fisher folk,
Singers and dancers,
Musicians and artisans.

Narrating blood and sweat
Tears and toil
Delight and peace,
A thousand souls
Fed each day
Rice for hungry bellies,
Prayers for famished hearts
None left hungry.

And a thousand years later,
A nation's father

Quenched his thirst -
When these gates
Embraced the untouchable
'People of God'.

Raja Raja, Shiva maniac
Carries Kailasha to Tanjore -
Shrines, tunnels, caverns
Stone softened to silk
Centuries of footsteps.

Amid granite, marble,
Bronze, brass,
Copper, silver and gold
Towers, turrets and spires -
Sun in the Milky way, Nandi,
Filled with the universe's strength
Shiva's mighty mount
Bearer of a million prayers
Whispered into bull ears
For ten thousand years.

Ganesha and Murugan
Guarding their father's shrine
Omnipresent, omniscient
At entrances, exits
And a myriad
Shrines overflowing
Vermilion, flowers, butter lamps.

Shiva's eternal beloved
In all her forms
Shivani, Annapurna, Uma

Parvati, Durga, Mahakali
Tender and terrible,
Subduing the lord of ascetics
Shakti consuming cosmos.

Devas, Asuras,
Apsaras, Rakshasas,
Animals, Humans,
Spirits good and evil,
All in Shiva, Shiva in all -
Brahma the creator
and
Vishnu the nurturer
Meditate upon
Shiva the destroyer,
Here, in Tanjore.


At the heart
Of a million universes
A limitless Linga
Sanctum Santorum
Core of creation
Womb of sacredness
Faith reaches
Fathomless peaks
Endless offerings
Unceasing sorrows
Relentless devotees
Endless energy engulfing
Lampstands, flagpoles
Statues, arches,
Gardens, pavements

Mandapas, mantras
Prayers, scriptures
Sermons, stories
Chatter, laughter
Tears, generations
All races.

Everyone here
Is divine -
Calm outside
Crazed inside
Swirling amid
Shiva's eternal
Icy flames.

Raja Raja, seeking to capture all His forms!?
Nataraja, divine dancer setting the universe's rhythm
Umasahitha Shiva, enslaved to his soulmate
Mahesha Shiva, God of gods and lord of lords
Chandrashekhara, bearer of the brilliant moon
Bhikshatana, monk, sage, mendicant,
Living in wilderness amid funeral pyres
Kalari, timeless lord and destroyer of death
Gangadhara, bearer of mighty Ganga's sacred flow
Dakshinamurthy, the supreme teacher,
Unravelling oceans of knowledge and wisdom.

Myriad Dynasties
Cholas post,
Sultans, Rajahs
Marathas, French, British
All seeking to protect
And possess

Rajarajesvaram -
Gateway of eternity.
Portals into multiverses
Hidden in unlikely nooks and corners
You might step into another dimension
Or enter other worlds
Or fly through the cosmos
Showered by infinite peace
Absence of all thought
Sweet empty sleep
Or perhaps
Find your own self.

Gods need mortals
Kings subjects;
Raja Raja's toiling millions
Got Tapeshwara to Tanjore;
And to this moment,
Nandisha seeks faith amid
Faceless hordes;
King and God
indebted to
Nameless
Devotee.

*(Note: In memory of a visit to the world famous Brihadeeshwara Temple in Tanjore, Tamil Nadu, South India.)*

# Velankanni

All the sorrow of the world
Rushes to your feet, Mother.
Hearing of agony is one thing
Seeing so much of it, unbearable.

Stick-thin pilgrims walk barefoot
Fathomless faith-filled miles
Shielded only by icons and images
Of you, Mother -
Adorned with
Hand-made flags, slum-made garlands,
And priceless sighs
Birthed by dark despair.

August and September
Are the cruellest months
Entire villages and towns obsessed
With you Virgin Mother,
With your sorrows and theirs -
Unending, undeserved.

A million sword-pierced hearts
Bleeding love
Refusing to learn the ways of the world.
Sorrow is their ornament

The fetter that sets them free
To fall into your arms Mother.

Bruised, ruby-red feet,
Crushed fingers, kneeling knees on burning sands
Proudly crawling to you Mother -
Silken soul in iron world.
In memory of favours received and to be received,
They give you gold and silver and pearl robes,
Coconuts, candles, flowers,
Pennies and the hair of their heads,
Prayers, chants, hot tears,
Because you need nothing.

Queen of all Universes
What do you lack?
Mother of all Sorrows
Who can comfort you?
Bridger of earth and heaven
What miracle greater than you?

Why did you call me here, Mother?
To burn my heart anew
To rip apart wretched scars
Or let festering wounds bleed afresh?
Old grudges, unheard prayers,
Unfulfilled dreams,
Unbearable injustice,
Not that you haven't stood by me,
But this cross grows too heavy.

Yet, my tears fall
For other broken hearts

And myriad desperate voices
Piercing the skies.
One earth-shattering howl
Bursts the depths of humbled souls -
"Hail Mary!"
Fishermen to filthy rich
You have no favourites -
Only here, do the grieving triumph
This is the kingdom of the poor
The realm of the persecuted
The feast of the unfortunate.

No power works here
Except that of belief and love.
Priests, prayers, rituals, holiness,
Blessings at a price
Everything falls apart,
Before the lady with a child
Clothed in sun, stars
And boundless compassion.

Compassion is your gift to me,
Mother
I return, forgetting self,
Remembering universal sorrow
Gathering mercy dew.
Crosses cannot be taken away,
Only
They can be made
Too sweet not to bear.
*(Note: Velankanni in Tamil Nadu, South India, houses a world-famous shrine and pilgrimage centre dedicated to Mother Mary.)*

## Avatar

He is anger
Pain
Rejection
And bitterness,
All rolled into one
Until
They turn to
Apathy.

Oblivious to good or bad
Criticism or praise
Present or Future
He moves around
Listening to no one
Not even himself.

He has decided to fail gloriously
To rebel in style
For no reason
But to spite the man and woman
That brought him into this world

And then fought over him
Tearing him
 Into a thousand pieces
That can never be
Put together again.

## Equaliser

Shall I speak of three ages in one age?
Three nations in one?
Or three worlds in one world?

The toiling peasant's child
Will sit on mud floors
Begin learning what the rest of the world has finished
Just enough to toil like enslaved fathers and mothers
Unless some phoenix arises
Stopping at nothing less than everything.

The billionaire's offspring
Will study in marble palaces
Accessing knowledge at a price none can pay
No door closed
As long as wealth can open it
All will rule the world
Handed to them on platinum spoons,
Seasoned and cut into dainty pieces.

Middle-class larvae
Caught like their parents
Between heaven and hell

Will have neither.
Average in all, midway they will stop
Clones of millions before and after them
Never venturing out of comforting delusions
Designed to please the world
Not their own selves.

All three worlds
Their own glories and failures
Some, knowledge without compassion
Others, goodness without strength.

All fine
Except when you tell your kids
Life is a race
Won by the hard worker
From so unfair a starting line?!

One equaliser for all
Innocence at the beginning
Sorrow at the end
Always Inescapable.

## Innocence at Eighteen

Clutching a cuddly doll,
I grew out of my innocence.
It makes no sense,
Now, to recall lost days and all,

Rosy, rosy dreams,
Reduced to dry, dry dust.
Whom should I trust?
My soul screams,

In remembrance sweet,
Of teddy bears and trusted hands,
Of carefree days and fairy-lands,
And summers without the heat,

That is now unbearably hot.
When I was a kid,
Joy could never be hid,
And sorrow was not,

Something easily found.
Life was one huge chocolate bar,
I knew little about bio war,
Which now like a fierce grey hound,

Stares me in the face.
From light to darkness,
From bliss to unhappiness,
Strange are life's ways.

I am an adult now,
Freshly baked at eighteen,
Introduced into a new routine,
I don't know why or how,

But I have arrived.
Into the world of actuality,
The universe of bitter reality-
An ugly secret, specially contrived,

For many like me.
I realize, rainbows can't be touched,
But hearts can be crushed;
That, 'to be or not to be',

Depends on fate,
On might and influence,
And, of course, my bank balance.
I understand people can really hate,

And be really nasty.
I realize, my kindergarten teachers weren't
philosophers,
Just common sinners.
I bet, I was hasty,

In drawing my childish conclusions.
Now I know, the loveliest rose withers,

The dearest friend falters.
I was living amongst horrible illusions,

Of eternal love and undying devotion.
Happy-endings are reserved for fairy tales,
Daily life feels like sharp, rusty iron nails.
I know it; there is no place for emotion.

My idols have crumbled,
My ideals shaken,
My heart broken,
I look down at icons that tumbled.

You know, you feel a little bad,
When your heroes turn ignoble,
When your own are no longer lovable;
It's indeed sad,

To know that greed and passion,
 Have always ruled;
That the fire of virtue was always cooled,
And hypocrisy was never out of fashion.

My eyes have been opened;-
Santa Claus doesn't exist, the atom bomb 'does',
Wisdom is scarce, men are 'callous',
Indeed, I have been enlightened.

I have learnt many things-
Mother's bosom can't banish 'all' fear,
Father's arms can't defeat evil 'here',
I'm just stretching my new wings.

Life is not all candy floss;
The tragedy of infidelity, unrequited love,
The bonds of here and now,
The fear of loss.

Childish laughter echoes from the 'past'
Can't laugh and dance and sing,
Can't spend the day on an old swing;
You have to be really 'fast',

Prim an' proper, formal, 'successful',
Gloating over science and 'modernity',
While naked, pot-bellied kids stare at you from
the confines of 'poverty';
You should be 'grateful',

To live in a world at war with itself,
Where vulgarity is valued,
Dishonesty praised,
Where the best are the saddest,
Where compromise is 'the' password,
And Innocence Is Formally Crushed
At Eighteen.

## Just One Prayer

Worship becomes woe
Faith turns fanatic
Religion looks revolting.
Hearts, minds, souls
Friends, families
Skin, bones
Life blood
Dissected
Divided
Butchered.
Then, just one prayer
To be
Religionless
Stateless
And
Godless.

# Manipur

Same story always
Unbearable beauty and terror
Co-existing.
But, this time,
New milestones -
Pitting tribe against tribe
Old religions against new
Customs against traditions
Majorities against minorities
Reasons never known fully
Effects are brilliant
Homes, churches, schools razed
Women paraded naked
Protesting menfolk
Shot dead instantly
Amid cries of 'Glory to Mother India'
The devil hangs his head in shame.

But, all is well now,
The fire had to burn
Those who had to be burnt
Would be beneath any leader to douse it
Those who ignite the spark
Have full peace of mind
They who give orders never kill.

As life disappears from a million homes
They gather every class and creed
In blood-red marble palaces
to celebrate

A Great Christmas
Without Christ.

## Memories

We live in the past,
The present seems dead,
The future is too fragile,
Vanishing before we visualise.
From the faint lingering warmth
Of ancient embraces,
Out of the fading imprints
Of old sight-seeing journeys,
Over the scanty fragrance of
The free breaths we took aeons ago,
We fight to live.
Even as we lose count
Of fallen warriors,
Most stoic, most devout
Struggle for hope.
Every home filled with fear,
Every heart soaked in sorrow,
Every body downright drained.
Death sweeps through
Once beautiful lands
Filling waters with corpses
Air with poison.
Prisoners in our own houses,
Separated from most of what we cherish,
We cling on to the feather
That can give us new life -
Memories.

*(Note: Written during the deadly second wave of the COVID-19 pandemic in India.)*

# Middle-Class Indian Memories

Whither or whence without memories?
Happy or sad
Always beautiful,
Carrying me
On life's roller-coaster wings
Intoxicated.

Old gold childhood
Rajdoot motorcycles
Fiat Premier Padminis
Father drove us around proudly in.
Mother's fried delicacies
Topped with gajar ka halwa.
Treasures parents returned home with
Cadbury Gems, Five Stars, Dairy Milk chocolates, Parle biscuits.
Dolls named and dressed every morning.
Which diamond will fetch those days?

Endless love affairs with libraries
Western fairy tales and Eastern folk tales
Akbar, Birbal, Tenali Rama,
Phantom, Superman
Famous Five, Nancy Drew
Sherlock Holmes and Feluda,

Shakespeare for Children and Reader's Digest for adults
Consumed in hiding with a ravenous heart

Summer holidays amid desert coolers,
Mango pickles and
Mother's vanilla-coffee ice-creams
The fragrance of her saris,
The feel of father's arms.

Churches frequented with childish requests,
Seeking miracles in every statue
School in the scent of rain and new books
Inspiring teachers, craft classes under huge trees,
Basketball games and eloquent speeches,
Fests and parades, cruel envy and silent scheming

A whirlwind called college
First trips, phones, crushes, diaries
Winter morning classes, huge gardens
English dramas and Hindi songs
Kachoris, jujubes, girls and boys
Fighting to be an art student
Soaking in the love of pet dogs
University days,
Lost in book shops, saree fairs,
Romantic dreams and road trips

Christmas cribs and plum cakes,
Diwali ladoos and diyas,
Easter buns and Ganpati puran polis,

First job, first book
First dreams and first promises
To change the world

Mountain memories
Of seas, forests, rivers, flowers, elephants,
Forts, palaces, foreign lands,
Nature's immortal bliss

Love's first fiery touch
First embrace and first tears
First gain and first loss,
Engraved in soul blood

Ambition, betrayal, tragedy
Of a million unfulfilled dreams
Murderously beautiful memories
That come to all
But give life only to a few?
Questions without answers

Sly memory
Brings me a silk saree or a story book
A picture I drew or a look
From loving eyes
A coffee or a cake or fresh lemon juice from mother's hands
The scent of rain drops on dry earth
Teacher father's smile reflected on my students' faces
Sister's sister talk,
Lover's laughter
And I forget everything
Except for the memory of
Pure joy.

## Moon Song

Ever old and ever new
Mother of a million nights
Virgin daughter of evening skies
Bathing in light
Eden evenings
And Himalayan heights
Companion to nightingales and lovers
Poets and painters
From Arabia to Anglia.
Magicking India's marble monuments
Churning Eastern oceans
Illuminating Kangaroo country
And Westward voyages.
Yet,
Tonight
A mute witness
To malicious might.
Woe-filled watcher
Of warring worlds,
On nights filled
Not with love or hope or peace
Or inspiration or dreams
Only endless evil.
Wherever I look
I see smoke, fire, blood

Out of the rubble of two great towers
A million lifeless eyes stare at me
And
A million sighs
Tear at me.
*(Note: originally conceived and written soon after the 9/11 tragedy.)*

## Post Truth

Who are we?
Walking, talking lies?
Well-dressed, well-decked zombies?
Permanent actors
With masks
Stitched to our souls.

Perhaps,
It's safe to be like this -
The light blinds us
Clean air can choke us
And pure water could burn us.

We no longer need reality
With a soulmate in AI
And a philosopher in ChatGPT.

The truth has died
Laughing at
The heights
 We have reached.

## Spy Versus Soldier

Both of us chose
To live
A little differently
and
A little more
Than the rest of them.

You chose to stand out
I, to blend in.
You will wear the flag and the stripes
The medals and the uniforms
The berets and batons,
With pride.
I will keep all hidden
In some dark corner,
My medals pinned in closed rooms
Bereft of ceremony
With no photographs to show my children.
Your name would be emblazoned everywhere
Chanted proudly by generations.

I live in false names, false passports, false documents
Changing a thousand times each day
Forgetting my own self,
My family, friends, likes and dislikes.

You take the bullet on the chest, unmoved
Yours will be a state funeral
Viewed by millions,
Children and streets and memorials will be named
after you.
Bullets will riddle my body too
Worse, crush my mind and tear my soul apart
But the moment I perish
My nation will dispose me off
Like dangerous nuclear waste
Disowned by countrymen
Humiliated by enemies
Branded a traitor
Ending an unidentified body
Who will name their children after me?
This nameless candle
Secretly burning out
To light many lives.

You chose your passion, soldier
I, spy, chose more than that
You offered body and mind
I, body, soul, heart, mind, identity, existence
Everything,
In return for
Ridicule, ingratitude, rejection
and
Worst of all,
Eternal Anonymity.

Even gods
Demand their dues;

I, greater than all,
Go silently,
Without expectations,
Bearing Bitter Punishment
For Selfless Service.

## Tiger at Tirumala

On the forested path
To the timeless
Mountain temple
Of a famous god
Befriended by
Beggars and billionaires,
Last month,
A tiger took away
The pilgrim child
Of a penniless clan.
She was just
Four or five,
Her parents say,
Numbers don't matter for
Those who cannot count.
The blame game starts
Sinners masquerading as saints:
Rulers, politicians,
Protectors, whistle-blowers.
The mother laments
Cursing the universe
The father sits,
Stoic.
Accusations ascend
Human intruders?

Overprotected animals?
Careless parents?
Merciless fate?
Systemic failure?
No one sees
The gleaming truth
Of one tender tiger,
Divinely ordained
To end in
The swift and
Soft jungle way
A tiny life destined for
Endless misery
In the inhuman
Company of
Human beings.

(*Note: In August 2023, a six-year-old girl named Lakshita was attacked by a tiger while walking on the Alipiri Walkway in Tirupati forests, on the famous pilgrimage to Tirumala Temple, South India.*)

## Two Worlds

Within these twelve months
I have taught kids who
Sat on stone floors
For want of benches
And kids whose trash
Sat in plush lockers
Kids whose intelligent questions
Were silenced by sticks
And kids whose rude remarks
Were encouraged as intelligence
Kids whose beings lit up
At the sight of food once a week
And kids who were begged
Not to waste delicacies thrice a day
Kids who fought over pencils and scrap
And kids who discarded designer brands
Kids who cleaned the streets
And kids who mocked
Those who tidied up after them
Kids who escorted me to the school gates
Holding me aloft on love waves
And kids who neither
Looked at me nor made way
Ready to push me down
 If I wasn't careful

Kids who would remember
Me all their lives
Though most would die poor
And a few would rule the world
And kids who would forget me
In less than an hour
For money would push them
To plush pastures.
I see them
Worlds apart with
Kindred joys and sorrows
Neglected, misguided,
Misunderstood
In different ways
The same innocence
And the same potential
Sometimes hidden
Sometimes evident
Give me wings
Make me a child
That I may give to each
In body, mind,
Heart and soul
That despair of poverty
And smug arrogance of riches
Might not destroy human future
That their innocence
Might rise and shine
Like a million stars
In every universe.

# Unfair

All our toil to end in predestined failure
Clinging hopes shattered into permanent despair;
Family to turn strangers and friends to foes
No painfully nurtured relationship
To be stronger than lamps in hurricanes
Soulmates, better halves – you will either fade
Into oblivion or betrayal or dust.
It is all decided –
Which honest man shall be slaughtered
Which black heart shall be deified.
The unlucky freak failures of unfortunate talent
The amazing rise of undeserving scoundrels
The innocent success of happy-go-luckies
The heartbroken sighs of sincere damned toilers
Everything is counted.
Except –
The length of our sorrows
The brevity of our joys
Ages spent with monsters
Seconds with angels.
And all this, for a candle-breath
Blown out without warning.

## Waiting to be Refuted

When the river is frozen, how do you swim?
Is writing one poem per day
Enough to fool yourself?
Does suffering without
Cause or limit ensure fame?
When medicine turns to poison
And every door, window
And crack in the wall close tight,
Does it make you a philosopher?
Or a character in a happy fairy tale?
Or the heroine of a rags-to-riches story?
In an unfair world filled with unfairer people
Does fairness ever count?
Teacher, teach skills
Not values
Skills to slay
Souls and mates
Values lead you to
No where
Except
Deep despair.
I would love
To be
Proved wrong
For once,
Please.

*Woman*

## Shackles

Freedom is a distant dream
When patriarchy seems immortal
Perpetuated fervently by its victims
When each female breath
Is grudged and dissected
When hard-won rights
Are paraded as favours.
Ruthlessness alone
Razes ruthlessness.
Some of us
Must become
Lesser than women,
So that
All of us
Can become
Complete women.

## Deep Brown Ocean

I am not the sunny-blue lake
You would love to swim in
Nor the shallow,
Chlorinated, fancy pool
Perfect for pictures.
I, not even a river,
That has its beginning, end
And markers of danger.
I am the ocean
Not calm and blue
But murky, deep brown,
Angry, mixed with sand and mud
Both from the beaches
And the fathomless deeps.

I am the one
You think you know
But you never really know.
Not appealing, but powerful
Not soothing, but meaningful.
I have swallowed
All your darkness
Borne all your pain.

Look at me, man,
I am your
Ego-crushing truth
Soul-searing solace
I have let you win,
You cannot bear loss
I have glorified my sorrow,
You can never bear
The pain you inflict.

I, the brown woman
Not exalted
Not famous or infamous
Like white or black or yellow.
I am staple food, air you breathe
Sunshine and water
I am not special.

Just
One more thing.
You are
Because
I am.

# The Disrobing of Draupadi

(As narrated by her maid, because
every Draupadi cannot afford a Krishna.)

This is a dark, dark day,
Darker than the darkest night.
Weep for a princess, weep for a woman,
O! weep at her plight.


Hail! land of Hastinapur,
Peerless paradise in Bharat's bosom.
Such is thy grandeur,
The gods look down from the sky
And ask why
Thou art holier than heaven.


Five Pandavas,
To match a hundred Kauravas.
Scholars, sages, warriors-hark!
Two queens of great divinity,
A blind monarch.
All proud rulers of one great city.

But today is a dark, dark day,
Darker than the darkest night.
Weep we at Draupadi's plight;
Noble princess, blue-blooded, beautiful,
Trapped in a terrible fight,
Among the godly sons of Kunti,
And the greedy offspring of Gandhari.

Princess of Panchal, Wife to not one ,
Wife to five peerless princes;
Pride of her clan,
Mesmerizer of the senses.

But today is a dark, dark day,
Turn your steps away
From the palace door;
Today Draupadi is victim for sure
To a scheming Shakuni's snare.
Today Panchali will mourn,
For her husbands love gambling,
And Duryodhana loves grabbing ,
What is not his own.

A simple plot,
To drive out Pandu's sons,
A game of dice to be held,
In full court

Dharmaraj distraught,
Blinded by despair,
Pawns his precious wife,
Loses her to a villain's care.

But today is a dark, dark day;
Draupadi is summoned twice,
Turn your eyes away,
The Kauravas exhibit their gambled prize.

Gandhari's eldest son,
Will have his revenge
She smiled her Swayamvar smile,
She did scorn him for a while.
Now, he'll drag her by her hair;
He could not shoot the revolving fish,
He'll hold her in his lap, it's his wish.

Dusshasana, vilest of all;
The chosen man,
To fulfill,
Duryodhana's desire and Shakuni's plan.

Dusshasana, drags her
Drags her by those long locks
By those locks of lustrous black
Of flaming black hair
Fie! Shame! Away, away!
This, a black day.

A blacker day will never dawn,
Dusshasana is pulling away,
Pulling away her robes,
Her robes at Duryodhan's behest,
Henceforth, Hastinapur won't rest;
Draupadi is being disrobed.

In full court, Draupadi stripped,
Amid scholars, knowledge ripped,
Amid warriors, bravery shamed,
Amid sages, sanctity tamed.


Will the rulers rise?
A princess murdered.
Will the scholars condemn?
Nobility stifled.
Will the warriors fight?
Dignity hanged.

No, no, no!
Draupadi screams and shudders
But, the men of learning and wisdom,
Those heirs of power and kingdom,
Those custodians of intuition and insight,
Even Bhishma does not fight.

Lowered eyes won't suppress the soul,
Mute mouths won't silence guilt,
Do what thou wilt…
The chronicles will say,
Tomorrow and Today,
They had eyes
But refused to see,
They had life
But refused to be.
They had ears,
But refused to hear,
They had tongues,
Too stiff to speak,

They had much strength,
Yet were weak.

My mistress implores,
How will they forget the sight,
Not one man deplores,
All cowards in the fight.

My mistress molested
Too much is my guilt,
Do what thou wilt
But I rise to defend,
The dignity of a woman.

Alas! My words can't be heard
Hands on my shoulders,
Fingers on my lips,
The great men are telling me,
Your mistress is fine,
Don't cry or whine,
Run out to the lawn,
Should you care for a pawn?

Draupadi in prayer,
Panchali calling her brother
Hark! Krishna-Murari, Madhava,
Devaki-Nandana, Gopala,
See Syama saving her sanctity,
Radheysham redeeming our humanity.

The Princess got her price,
Dusshasan's blood
To anoint her crown

Duryodhan's crushed thighs
To remove her frown.


But, listen, men of to-day,
This is a dark, dark day,
Darker than the darkest night.
Justice Disrobed
Truth Raped
From Kaurava Hastinapur
To Pandava Indraprastha
From Draupadi to
Thousand Nirbhayas
And Abhayas
Do you still

Enjoy the Sight ?

*(Note: Based on episodes from the Mahabharata and recent acts of violence against women.)*

## Lakshmi Bai

Will you remember her,
As she came bedecked for war?
All her life,
For this one moment
Preparing,
Covered in vermilion,
Golden sinews thirsting for victory,
She came and stood…
Strong, yet terribly weak.

Her whole existence
Centred on this one moment,
All her sorrows and joys
Trials and triumphs
Humiliation and pride
Misfortune and memories.

She was at the mercy of the moment.
Or, was the moment at her mercy?

Will you remember her,
 She was no saint,
Not a goddess
- Very human, made of darker earth.
Not very beautiful
Yet redefining beauty.
Those deep black eyes

Upturned lashes
Quivering, generous lips
A raised forehead like majesty itself
An exquisite chin –
Delicate like the flowers
Strong as steel

No, she was not too lovely.
No doe-eyes
Or aquiline nose
No blushing cheeks,
Yes, the brows were always arched
In question and in defiance
In laughter or in grief.
Long hair cascaded to the waist
Dark and straight, jet-black
No curls, no twists, all plainness
An unredeemed Draupadi.

She was not a princess
Though they sometimes said
She had blue blood in her veins.
Not some Snow-White.
Not a Helen.

But, you could never forget those intense eyes,
That saw you through and through,
Looked at you and transfixed you,
Spoke of fearless, shameless audacity,
Of Sita's loyalty and Razia's rebellion,
Of Radha's love and Savitri's courage.
Once in an age,
When she laughed,

O they were too bright to bear,
Sparkling like sunlit diamonds.
Perhaps, that is why,
She never laughed often.
Those eyes were her souls-
Filtering every feeling
Trapping all pain and bliss.

Will you remember her,
As she stood,
Defeated in life, Victorious in death.
She, finally, as she came to know-
Life is Maya
Victory lies in unquestioning acceptance
In contentment
Not in endless striving;
In defiance of fate
Not in cringing desire;
In unexpecting apathetic excellence;
Running the race to the very end
Forgetting about victory.
Accepting gloom and gladness
Ecstatic gain and searing loss
With the
Same
Indifference.

Fighting till she fell.
The Earth-Goddess.
The bravest of the brave.*

(*When the Rani of Jhansi fell fighting the British, the British generals remarked, " The bravest of the brave has fallen.")

# The Phoenixes of Bombay

Burnt, butchered
Bludgeoned, betrayed
Resurrecting from blood and ashes
Cut up, cast away
Divided, doomed
Re-writing history
Their way.

Asked to kill
For religion
They preferred death
To backstabbing
Raped and starved
Homes burnt and dear ones sliced up
They rose to offer
Honour and food and home
Learning and living
And hope to thousands of thirsty hearts.

Repaying hate with love
War with peace
Ignorance with knowledge
And extremism with
A heart
Embracing the universe.

*(Note: Dedicated to the ordinary women of Bombay who rose to fight for peace amid the terrible riots of 1992-1993)*

*Survival*

## A Fine Balance

Dancing gracefully
Without protest
With a smile
On the tightrope
Between
Love and hate
Laughter and tears
Selflessness and selfishness
Hope and despair
Bitter failure and ruthless fate
Trust and treachery
Compassion and cruelty
Life and death
I have fallen from the sky
A hundred times;
Surviving
Only because
Someone
Had softly spread
My dreams
On the ground.

## Evasion

Sweet, silent sleep,
Soft slumber,
Embrace me;
I need to rest.

    Tarry not,
    Come swiftly on eagle's wings,
    My weary eyes yearn,
    For the comfort your touch brings.

Divine enchantress,
Bear me into thy charmed castle.
Let me dream and die,
Die and dream-
Endless, ceaseless dreams-
Dipped in honey, bathed in rainbows,
Wrapped in thornless roses.

    Come sleep come,
    This world is filled with heartless scum,
    With righteous men gone wrong,
    With cruel beauty and joyless song.

Merciful goddess,
May I ever rest in thy bosom;

Not on this earth,
Which has no dearth,
Of broken hearts and shattered dreams.
Lend me some sweet solace,
Of loveliest dreams that'll never end,
And nightmares that'll never be.
Pity my plight,
And let me alight,
Ship-wrecked on thy silent shores;
I know nothing.
I need to rest.

## How Easy

You, me, and the boundless ocean,
How tempting
To walk in royally
With a fiery embrace
And a passionate kiss
And end all petty existence.

Until microscopic crabs
And
Finger-size turtle babies
Mock me,
Squaring it out alone
With enormous waves
And fathomless deeps.

Who says you can't beat the wind?
Try becoming the whirlwind...
With a fiery embrace
And a passionate kiss.

## Lent to Lent

Every passing summer brings
Lesser time for longer diary entries
Eloquent prose degenerates to lacklustre poetry
As I offer up my worthless suffering every
Good Friday.
What has changed?
Everything. Nothing.

In my 'democratic' country, freedom dies a
little more
Each day, with every change of rulers.
The rich teach us a new morality
The powerful shape our destinies
Young men of great merit gladly hang
themselves
The rest are in prison for high treason.
Is it not sedition to expose the plutocracy?
To bare the dark acts of white-skinned
nationalists?
Remember, silence is best if you
Are a poor man of any creed,
Or any woman from anywhere,
Or any kind of minority: agewise, thoughtwise
or actwise.

Now, may I turn inwards?
Lift the lovely curtain
And show the hideous scabs within?
Ugly scars and gaping wounds where
Love and innocence
And a thousand sparkling dreams once lived.
All washed clean; the marks refuse to go.
One must be careful -
Certain sights and sounds, certain types of weather,
Glimpses of beauty, old memories, old songs, old voices,
Old friends, happy times,
Success stories,
These are to be avoided.
Any of these can trigger
The fatal infection of hope
The pus of desire
And soul bleeding.
Reality's the best antiseptic
Despair, the dearest disinfectant.

One problem remains unresolved
The terror that fills you at dawn
Treasured people fading away into eternity
The death of merit, of goodness, of a new dream each day
Fear of loneliness, of oblivion, of a life labelled 'worthless'.

Show me a way out -
Free from desire, one day of 'living'.
Remember the girl

Who died unknown
Her beautiful beginnings, her glorious dreams,
Her quenched fire, her lost battles,
Carry them onward,
Who knows, someone else might
Live and
Win.

## Long Drive

On the long drive of life,
I must come to you, my friend.
Drowning in you, every now and then,
Driving a silver-grey sedan,
On autumn mornings turning to winter,
Through your hills and valleys,
By your windswept beach-bound highways.
Everything has changed,
Except for you -
As mysterious, as overwhelming, as comforting
As ever.
One winter, I met goodness by your side,
This autumn, I fight darkness, with you beside.
When I was a child, I saw you defeating the land,
Now, I see your waves struggling with mere sand.
All sea and sky are one blue grey now,
All one, no separating lines.
This calm kills me.
Tsunami, tornado, typhoon, or cyclone -
Make me any one, my friend!
Let us bring back old innocence,
And all else,
Rage and Raze.

## No Greater Peace

When the universe is
At war with itself
In a hostile world
Embellished with hostile hearts
Darkness feeding on souls
With every ray of light
Under attack
Then no greater peace
Than to come home.

Tiny haven of huge brightness
Absorbing sorrow seas
Into a harmony of hearts.

Hope roof over humble walls
Faith-filled food of love
Old age enchants
Youth sparkles
And animals teach humanity.

Desires, wealth, fame,
Luxury, ambition, success -
One by one, struck off the list.

When soul survival is at stake,
Body, mind, heart
Recede into the shadows.

What remains is a
First Painful
Then Peaceful
Choice –
"Home Truth".

## Of Not Making It

Behind all the glamour and shine
The fake smiles
The make-believe busy routine,
Behind the futile attempts
To occupy and to be occupied,
Lies a fear, refusing to part.
The horror of having to accept defeat
Effacing every effort,
Of being punished in the end
For just One fault
Palliating previous perfection.
Unfair race against unequal rivals
Foolish combat with frozen fate
Amid lasting grief and a mirage called joy.
After a million efforts,
An iota of success,
Mocked and swallowed at once
By a monstrous universe.
Everything obliterated
By the deep black
Indelible, overflowing
Ink
Of
Failure.

# Return to School

When I return to you
After two decades,
Having walked the straight and narrow path of
Mindless sincerity and fruitless hard work
Wrong choices to stay back in wrong places
In a wrong land, with wrong people,
Accomplishing nothing
Except for a clear view of failure
How should I feel?

I dare not enter
I dare not be seen
Living incognito
Barely surviving on fake identities and past laurels
I visit on a Sunday sunset when no one is around
Roaming through the darkening grounds.

My past meets me at every turn
My big successes in that small school
My lofty dreams of a small age
Cackle like mocking witches from the shadows
Childhood innocence sits forlorn,
Weeping under the ancient trees
That alone remain unchanged.

For all my work and glory,
My name could not be engraved
On your portals
That privilege belonged to others.

Quietly, I turn around before
The light fades
Totally.
Look at you
And make a promise.
Shall not run away
Shall keep haunting you
In disguise
Until you engrave my name on your walls
Until I stand on this podium
Where I have given
A hundred fiery speeches
Speak again to your students
Telling them
All is never lost
For
Those who walk
The straight and narrow path
In a crooked world.

## Shattered

They stick out of me
Like a hundred glass-shards.
Old knives and nails
Piercing
Flesh and soul,
Hurt no longer.
Only those who see me
Are affected.
I laugh
To see
Other
Shattered dreamers.

## That Whereby Men Live

Night must end
And dazzling sun dawn.
Light must shine
Amid laughter and wine.
Wars end
And flowers bloom.
Peace to prevail
And foes to fail.
Victory, even in the last breath,
Believing in new life after death.
For
Hope is that Whereby Men Live.

## Black Eagle Books

www.blackeaglebooks.org
info@blackeaglebooks.org

Black Eagle Books, an independent publisher, was founded as a nonprofit organization in April, 2019. It is our mission to connect and engage the Indian diaspora and the world at large with the best of works of world literature published on a collaborative platform, with special emphasis on foregrounding Contemporary Classics and New Writing.

www.ingramcontent.com/pod-product-compliance
Lightning Source LLC
Chambersburg PA
CBHW060608080526
44585CB00013B/738